DATE DUE

DEMCO 38-296

INVENTIONS AND DISCOVERY

Jonas Salk and the Polio Vaccine

by Katherine Krohn

illustrated by Al Milgrom

Consultant:
David Oshinsky, PhD
Author of *Polio: An American Story*
Department of History
University of Texas at Austin
Austin, Texas

Capstone *press*

Mankato, Minnesota

Graphic Library is published by Capstone Press,
151 Good Counsel Drive, P.O. Box 669, Mankato, Minnesota 56002.
www.capstonepress.com

1 2 3 4 5 6 11 10 09 08 07 06

Library of Congress Cataloging-in-Publication Data
Krohn, Katherine E.
    Jonas Salk and the polio vaccine / by Katherine Krohn ; illustrated by Al Milgrom.
    p. cm.—(Graphic library. Inventions and discovery)
    Summary: "In graphic novel format, tells the story of Jonas Salk's involvement in the
development of a polio vaccine"—Provided by publisher.
    Includes bibliographical references and index.
    ISBN-13: 978-0-7368-6483-1 (hardcover)
    ISBN-10: 0-7368-6483-0 (hardcover)
    ISBN-13: 978-0-7368-7518-9 (softcover pbk.)
    ISBN-10: 0-7368-7518-2 (softcover pbk.)
    1. Salk, Jonas, 1914–1995. 2. Virologists—United States—Biography—Juvenile literature.
3. Poliomyelitis vaccine—Juvenile literature. I. Milgrom, A. (Allen), ill. II. Title. III. Series.
QR31.S25K76 2007
614.5'49092—dc22   2006008188

Designers
Jason Knudson and Juliette Peters

Colorist
Ken Steacy

Editor
Christopher Harbo

Editor's note: Direct quotations from primary sources are indicated by a yellow background.

Direct quotations appear on the following pages:
Page 16, from Dr. Thomas Francis' speech at the University of Michigan on April 12, 1955, as
    quoted in Jeffrey Kluger's *Splendid Solution: Jonas Salk and the Conquest of Polio* (New
    York: G. P. Putnam's Sons, 2004).
Page 18, from Dr. Jonas Salk's interview on the television program *See It Now* on April 12,
    1955, as quoted in Richard Carter's *Breakthrough: The Saga of Jonas Salk* (New York:
    Trident Press, 1966).

Table of Contents

Chapter 1

Respected Scientist 4

Chapter 2

Important Research 10

Chapter 3

National Hero 16

Chapter 4

A Safer World 24

More about Jonas Salk
and the Polio Vaccine 28

Glossary 30

Internet Sites 30

Read More 31

Bibliography 31

Index 32

Respected Scientist

In the first half of the 1900s, a disease called polio, or poliomyelitis, infected thousands of people in the United States. Polio, also known as infantile paralysis, mainly attacked children.

She woke up with a high fever and cramps. We need to get her to a doctor fast!

No, please! Not polio!

Polio attacked the spinal cord, sometimes killing its victims. Many who survived the disease were left paralyzed.

In severe cases, some victims were forced to rest in machines called "iron lungs" just to keep breathing.

Chapter 2

Important Research

To make the vaccine, Salk started with a live polio virus.

He killed the virus with a strong-smelling chemical called formaldehyde.

In December 1951, the NFIP gave Salk permission to do testing on 40 children with polio. Although his tests wouldn't cure the patients, Salk hoped to learn if his vaccine might work for people.

Thank you for going first.

I don't want any kids to go through what I have.

The children's blood samples were tested to see what type of the virus each child had.

Then the children received a vaccine made from their virus type.

Weeks later, blood samples were drawn again.

Back at the lab, the polio virus was then added to the new blood samples.

12

Meanwhile, polio was striking thousands of children each summer. Finally, in 1954 the NFIP gave Salk permission for a nationwide study. Dr. Thomas Francis was asked to evaluate the results of the study.

The vaccine will be shipped to 44 states. We expect more than a million parents to volunteer their healthy children to receive the vaccine.

Excellent. I look forward to reviewing the results.

Randy Kerr became the first "polio pioneer." He received the first vaccine in Salk's field study.

This will sting a little.

That wasn't so bad.

You're a brave boy!

PRESS

Chapter 3

National Hero

On April 12, 1955, Dr. Francis announced the results of the polio field study at the University of Michigan.

During the spring of 1954, Dr. Jonas Salk and his team did a large-scale field study of a polio vaccine. Today, the results are clear.

The vaccine works. It is safe, effective, and potent.

The crowd was stunned. Finally, Salk's polio vaccine would be available to people all over the country.

With this vaccine, children can have the summer back again. They no longer have to be afraid to swim together or play together.

News of Salk's vaccine spread quickly. Some cities had celebrations. Church bells rang and factory sirens wailed.

NEWSSTAND

Detroit News 5¢
POLIO BEATEN!
SALK SUCCEEDS

A few days later, President Dwight Eisenhower honored Dr. Salk and Basil O'Connor, director of the NFIP, at the White House.

Gentlemen, thank you for your groundbreaking work, which will benefit so many people.

Salk's vaccine was soon shipped across the country. The supply of vaccine was limited, but the government made sure young children and pregnant women received the vaccine first.

What's wrong?!

Haven't you heard? Your vaccine has been linked to 204 new cases of polio.

That's impossible!

What could have gone wrong?

I don't know. But I intend to find out!

Dr. Salk contacted the drug companies that made the vaccine.

I want a detailed description of the formula you used to make the vaccine—

—and I want it now!

Salk learned that one of the drug companies didn't follow his exact instructions to make the vaccine. The mistake allowed live polio virus to get into some of the vaccine.

It's not your fault, Dr. Salk.

Still, I feel terrible about it.

Once the problem was corrected, no one else got polio from the vaccine. Better yet, the vaccine quickly proved its effectiveness. In 1955, the United States reported 28,985 new cases of polio. One year later, the number of cases was cut in half. Two years later, the United States reported only 5,894 new polio cases.

Naturally, the excitement for polio shots wasn't shared by everyone.

Why do I have to get another polio shot? I've already had two!

You have one more booster shot to go. The vaccine is given in three shots.

Awww, mom!

While people in the United States were receiving the Salk vaccine, American scientist Dr. Albert Sabin was working on his own vaccine. Unlike Salk, Sabin believed a polio vaccine with a live virus would protect people better.

In 1959, Sabin conducted a field test of his live virus polio vaccine in Russia.

Chapter 4
A Safer World

Salk's success with the polio vaccine inspired him to open the Salk Institute for Biological Studies in La Jolla, California, in 1962.

I want my institute to be a place where scientists, chemists, and philosophers can work together.

Yes, and together we will seek out cures for diseases such as cancer and multiple sclerosis. It's a great goal, Dr. Salk.

27

More about
Jonas Salk and the
Polio Vaccine

Jonas Salk was born October 28, 1914, in New York City. His parents were Russian-Jewish immigrants. Although they couldn't afford to send him to college, Salk won scholarships to pay for his education. He graduated from New York University medical school in 1939.

In 1916, when Salk was just a toddler, the worst polio epidemic in history hit the United States. That year 6,000 people were killed by the disease. Another 27,000 people were left paralyzed.

About 1,830,000 children participated in Salk's 1954 field study. But not all of these children received the vaccine. Some children were given a shot made of sugar water and others received no shot at all. These children were part of the control group. The control group allowed researchers to compare polio infection rates between children who got the vaccine and those who didn't.

In the final stages of his polio research, Salk trusted his vaccine so much that he gave it to himself, his wife, and his children.

Polio wasn't a problem in just the United States in the early-1900s. Many other countries were also suffering large polio epidemics. By 1959, more than 90 countries were using Salk's vaccine to fight polio.

By 1962, Albert Sabin's polio vaccine replaced Salk's vaccine in the United States. Although many scientists believed Sabin's live virus vaccine was more effective, it caused about eight cases of polio each year. In 2000, the United States went back to using the Salk vaccine because a killed virus vaccine is safer.

Sabin and Salk disagreed about whether a killed virus or a live virus vaccine was more effective. Their debate caused them to become bitter rivals. Sabin once went so far as to say, "Salk was strictly a kitchen chemist. He never had an original idea in his life."

Jonas Salk died on June 23, 1995. After his death, other researchers carried on his work to fight deadly diseases at the Salk Institute.

GLOSSARY

antibodies (AN-ti-bahd-eez)—proteins made by the body that weaken or destroy invading bacteria, viruses, and poisons

immune system (i-MYOON SISS-tuhm)—part of the body that protects it from diseases by producing antibodies

paralyzed (PAIR-uh-lized)—unable to move or feel

patent (PAT-uhnt)—a legal document that gives an inventor the right to make, use, or sell an invention for a set period of years

vaccine (vak-SEEN)—dead or weakened germs injected into a person or animal to help fight disease

virus (VYE-ruhss)—a tiny particle that infects living things and causes diseases

INTERNET SITES

FactHound offers a safe, fun way to find Internet sites related to this book. All of the sites on FactHound have been researched by our staff.

Here's how:
1. Visit *www.facthound.com*
2. Choose your grade level.
3. Type in this book ID **0736864830** for age-appropriate sites. You may also browse subjects by clicking on letters, or by clicking on pictures and words.
4. Click on the **Fetch It** button.

FactHound will fetch the best sites for you!

READ MORE

Bankston, John. *Jonas Salk and the Polio Vaccine.* Unlocking the Secrets of Science. Bear, Del.: Mitchell Lane, 2002.

Durrett, Deanne. *Jonas Salk.* Inventors and Creators. Detroit: Kidhaven Press, 2002.

Hecht, Alan. *Polio.* Deadly Diseases and Epidemics. Philadelphia: Chelsea House, 2003.

McPherson, Stephanie Sammartino. *Jonas Salk: Conquering Polio.* A Lerner Biography. Minneapolis: Lerner, 2002.

Parks, Peggy J. *Jonas Salk: Polio Vaccine Pioneer.* Giants of Science. San Diego: Blackbirch Press, 2004.

BIBLIOGRAPHY

Carter, Richard. *Breakthrough: The Saga of Jonas Salk.* New York: Trident Press, 1966.

Kluger, Jeffrey. *Splendid Solution: Jonas Salk and the Conquest of Polio.* New York: G. P. Putnam's Sons, 2004.

Oshinsky, David. *Polio: An American Story.* New York: Oxford University Press, 2005.

Williams, Greer. *Virus Hunters.* New York: Knopf, 1959.

INDEX

American Medical Association (AMA), 23
animal testing, 11
antibodies, 6, 11, 13

booster shots, 22, 23

Eisenhower, Dwight D., 19

flu vaccine, 6–7
Francis, Thomas, 6–7, 14, 16

human testing, 11–13, 14, 22, 28

iron lungs, 4

Kerr, Randy, 14
killed virus vaccines, 6, 9, 10, 29

live virus vaccines, 6, 9, 10, 22, 23, 29

March of Dimes, 5
Murrow, Edward R., 18

National Foundation for Infantile Paralysis (NFIP), 5, 6, 7, 9, 12, 14, 19

nationwide field study, 14, 16, 28

O'Connor, Basil, 19

polio
    epidemics, 21, 28, 29
    other names for, 4
    symptoms of, 4, 27
    transmission of, 5
    types, 7, 8, 11, 12

Roosevelt, Franklin D., 5

Sabin, Albert, 22–23, 29
Salk, Jonas
    birth of, 28
    death of, 29
    education of, 28
    and flu vaccine, 6–7
    and polio vaccine research, 8–9, 10–13, 25
    and tainted vaccine, 20–21
Salk Institute for Biological Studies, 24, 29
sugar cube vaccine, 23

World Health Organization, 27